SUMMARY
of Michael A.
Singer's
THE
UNTETHERED
SOUL

The Journey Beyond Yourself

by SUMOREADS

Copyright © 2017 by SUMOREADS. All rights reserved.
This book or parts thereof may not be reproduced in any
form, stored in any retrieval system, or transmitted in any
form by any means—electronic, mechanical, photocopy,
recording, or otherwise—without prior written permission of
the publisher, except as provided by United States of
America copyright law. This is an unofficial summary and is
not intended as a substitute or replacement for the original
book

TABLE OF CONTENTS

Key Takeaway: Your mental chatter creates an alternate version of reality that causes your suffering.

Key Takeaway: Recognize and let go of the part of yourself at conflict with reality to find inner peace.

Key Takeaway: The journey beyond you self begins with self-observation

Key Takeaway: You are the consciousness that remains when everything you see, think, or feel fades away.

Key Takeaway: True meditation takes your Self from the finite to infinite.

Key Takeaway: You have unlimited access to infinite spiritual energy.

Key Takeaway: Stay open to immerse yourself in your Spirit.

Key Takeaway: Thoughts and emotions that don't pass through you block your Spirit.

Key Takeaway: Release your experiences to enjoy life.

Key Takeaway: Loosen your hold on your self-concept to find peace and spiritual growth.

Key Takeaway: Your definition of how things ought to be for you to be okay creates your suffering.

Key Takeaway: Center your consciousness in the seat of the witness to free yourself.

Key Takeaway: Observe your inner roommate's struggle to be okay and refuse to participate in it.

Key Takeaway: Stop asking your mind to make everything okay to be okay.

Key Takeaway: Embrace your inner pain to accelerate your spiritual growth.

Key Takeaway: Break the walls that lay a siege on your consciousness to find true freedom.

Key Takeaway: Disbelieve your mental model to find true spirituality.

Key Takeaway: Let go of your self-concept to find your true, free, and secure self

Key Takeaway: Commit to stay open to find and sustain happiness.

Key Takeaway: Nonresistance is the path to inner peace.

Key Takeaway: Regularly reflect on death to gain perspective.

Key Takeaway: Stick to the middle way to find and sustain clarity.

Key Takeaway: Release your conceptual self to move toward your spiritual being.

EXECUTIVE SUMMARY

In his book *The Untethered Soul: The Journey Beyond Yourself*, Michael A. Singer explores how a self-concept built on thoughts, emotions, and beliefs holds people back and explains how they can transcend their restricted selves, find inner peace and joy, and become one with the light of the universe.

Singer contends that true spiritual growth comes from realizing and reminding yourself that your inner voice—with all its fears and doubts—is not you and says nothing about you. Your true Self is the part of you that observes and manipulates your thoughts and emotions. When you see yourself as nothing more than an objective observer of your thoughts and emotions, as only the witness of your experiences, you center yourself in your consciousness and move toward true spirituality.

The Untethered Soul uncovers the energies that limit access to consciousness—the source of true freedom—and shows how anyone can release these energies, live in the present moment, and, consequently, free himself of his inner pain and suffering. It explains the human mind's constant struggle to acquire a sense of control and safety and proposes a way to surrender and immerse oneself in the peace of the Spirit.

PART I:
AWAKENING CONSCIOUSNESS

Key Takeaway: Your mental chatter creates an alternate version of reality that causes your suffering.

If you are like most people, you have a persistent inner voice that takes both sides of the conversations in your head. It is a perpetual judge that comforts and berates you, focuses and distracts you, believes and doubts you.

The purpose of mental chatter is to release the thoughts and emotions that build up in your head, to explain the world around you, and to manipulate your perception of the outside world in order to give you a sense comfort and control. The inner voice re-creates and operates in an alternate version of reality because reality is too raw, too ambiguous for comfort.

Your inner voice can't change your reality, but it can, and it often does, say things to make you feel better or worse about your past, present, and future circumstances.

The way to free yourself from this voice is to recognize that it is not you; it merely talks to you. True growth comes from the realization that the voice in your head says nothing about you. Only from this realization can you transcend the chatter that remodels your reality and prevents you from completely engaging with life.

"The truth is that most of life will unfold in accordance with forces far outside your control, regardless of what your mind says about it" (p. 10).

Key Takeaway: Recognize and let go of the part of yourself at conflict with reality to find inner peace.

You find inner peace and contentment when you quiet your mental chatter. Part of quieting this chatter is to realize that you are the witness—not the object—of your inner disturbance. From this perspective, you can shut out that part of you that imposes its opinion on everything.

Instead of asking yourself what you will do about a problem or unwanted emotion, ask yourself what part of you thinks it's a problem or is being bothered by the emotion. As long as you maintain this objective view of your problems, you can't get lost in them.

Key Takeaway: The journey beyond you self begins with self-observation.

Taking back control of your life from your psyche begins with observing it and recognizing how unreliable it is.

Imagine the source of your mental chatter—your psyche or inner roommate—is a physical being separate from you. Imagine it's a person talking to you. Let her talk, listen, and observe how capricious and neurotic she is. Recall how many times she has been wrong in the past and recognize that she's not trustworthy.

With sufficient self-observation, you will realize that your inner roommate is the one problem you have had all along.

Key Takeaway: You are the consciousness that remains when everything you see, think, or feel fades away.

You are the subject, and everything you see, hear, think, or dream is the object of your consciousness. Anything you can observe outside and inside of you, anything that can take your attention—the table in front of you, your body in the mirror, your physical experiences, your thoughts, and your emotions—is not you. You are what would remain if everything that passes by or inside you ceased to exist.

You are your consciousness—the part of you that is aware of the objects within and without you, the experiencer and manipulator of your thoughts. You are the part of you that is aware of your surroundings and emotions without having to think about them.

Key Takeaway: True meditation takes your Self from the finite to infinite.

When your dreams are lucid, you are aware that you are dreaming. The lucid Self can be understood along similar lines. This self is aware that it is aware—it knows it is the receiver of experiences, thoughts, and emotions. Because of this awareness, it is not lost in any of the thoughts or emotions it experiences.

You choose what to focus on with your conscious. When you let it roam, your conscious can focus on objects, experiences, thoughts, or emotions and lose its awareness of everything else. Your conscious can get so preoccupied with your thoughts, emotions, and the sights and sounds around you that it becomes one with them.

When you focus on objects, thoughts, or emotions too closely, they pull you in and absorb your consciousness. You become unaware that you are the one experiencing the objects, or thinking the thoughts, or feeling the emotions. When you lose awareness of your conscious, you lose the perception of yourself as the subject and perceive yourself as part of your experiences.

When you are centered—when your Self is lucid—you are aware of your consciousness as being independent of the objects around and within you. You are aware of your thoughts, aware of your awareness. The goal of true meditation is to get you to this level of awareness. It is to separate your consciousness from your experiences so that you can see the world and your problems objectively.

"The more you are willing to just let the world be something you're aware of, the more it will let you be who you are— the awareness, the Self, the Atman, the Soul" (p. 37).

PART II:
EXPERIENCING ENERGY

Key Takeaway: You have unlimited access to infinite spiritual energy.

You use energy to create and manipulate thoughts, to deal with emotions, and to act. This inner energy is separate from caloric energy. It is the energy that fills you when you are excited and dissipates when you are depressed.

Inner energy is infinite and always available to you. You cut yourself off from it when you close your chakras, your energy centers. When you open your heart—one of the energy centers—you open yourself to energy flows from deep within yourself—from your Chi, your Shakti, your Spirit. You open yourself to love, joy, boundless enthusiasm, and healing when you open your heart.

Key Takeaway: Stay open to immerse yourself in your Spirit.

To stay open, you simply need to remind yourself to not close. This self-reminder is most urgent when you encounter people or situations that made you close—made you feel angry, envious, or fearful—in the past.

Closing is a conscious choice. People close to protect themselves from external disturbances, but closing does not protect them from anything; it only cuts them off their energy sources. When you let go of the inner energies you are watching and embrace life and everything that happens to you, you open yourself to life and to your Spirit. In time, you forget to close.

You keep your energy sources open by maintaining conscious awareness of your inner roommate, making conscious effort to stay open, and meditating.

Key Takeaway: Thoughts and emotions that don't pass through you block your Spirit.

The heart is an energy center that opens and closes to energy flows. Depending on the energy flow it allows or restricts, you feel love, enthusiasm, inspiration, anger, and a range of other positive and negative emotions. You feel empty and depressed when your heart closes to everything.

The heart closes when unsettled energy patterns from the past block it. These unsettled energy patterns include hurtful experiences, unresolved feelings, and anything that takes your focus from the present. If you could live in the present, you would be perpetually open; you would find every moment exciting.

Thoughts that don't pass through you block your energy flow. Unresolved hurt, jealousy, resentment—even events that cause extraordinary joy—are blocked when you cling to them. These impressions or unfinished energy patterns are stored in the heart where they keep cycling. If they are not released, they lie dormant and are activated when you encounter the event that triggered them.

If thoughts could pass through you the way trees pass by you on the highway (without leaving any impression), you could feel your Spirit flow in and experience the infinite love and joy it holds.

Key Takeaway: Release your experiences to enjoy life.

The amount of love, joy, or inspiration you experience depends on how open you are—how much energy flows through you.

When you let go of your external experiences, you open yourself to a beautiful inner experience. Let the experiences of your life—both positive and negative—pass through you. Don't cling onto or fight them; let the energy of your impressions flow through. When a cue stimulates the pain bottled up from your past, relax your heart and let the pain pass through.

Key Takeaway: Loosen your hold on your self-concept to find peace and spiritual growth.

In the absence of physical threats to worry about, people have shifted their focus to psychological threats, the consequence of which has been hypersensitive egos. When you have a hypersensitive ego, any situation that elicits fear, anxiety, or any other sort of emotional discomfort cues you to put up a protective shield around your self-concept.

When you withdraw to protect your ego, you close your energy centers and imprison yourself in a self-made cage. As long as you protect yourself, you are never free. There's no room for growth.

The more you close yourself, the more it becomes the default coping mechanism to every disturbance you experience. To break from this cycle, pay attention to the part of you that tends to close and challenge it. Loosen your grip on your defenses, on your obsession over what people will think or do, and open yourself to whatever comes next.

You don't have to follow your thoughts or your disturbed energy with your consciousness. You can choose to observe as thoughts and energies come and go. Your conscious can't follow these energies unless you focus it on them. You feed your negative emotions when you pay attention to them.

Make a commitment to recognize when your energy changes. When something or someone threatens your self-concept—whenever you find yourself tightening up—breathe and release. Practice letting go of the small altercations that create your angst and inner freedom will be within your grasp.

PART III:
FREEING YOURSELF

Key Takeaway: Your definition of how things ought to be for you to be okay creates your suffering.

Your major struggle is not with your external circumstances but with your inner fears and insecurities. Fear is the source of jealousy, prejudice, and just about every negative emotion and problem you have. Fear breeds from the feeling that things are not the way they should be. Your attempts to make order out of a chaotic world, to define how the world ought to be in order to feel okay, get you farther away from the sense of control and safety you seek because the natural unfolding of life is unpredictable and uncontrollable.

You can either relinquish your need for control or protect yourself from situations that stimulate your fear, insecurity, and unease. When you try to protect yourself from fear or insecurity, you feed it and create more of it. The more you try to define how things should be, the more you avoid things that don't feel right, the more everything feels like a threat. Part of overcoming fear is accepting that life is constantly changing and opening your heart to everything that comes.

Key Takeaway: Center your consciousness in the seat of the witness to free yourself.

Your consciousness is attracted to anything that draws its attention or makes you uncomfortable. You can allow it to leave its witness seat and take the disturbance seat, or you can ground it so that it merely observes and lets the disturbance pass through. Centering your consciousness on the witness seat enables you to see everything objectively and to realize that your psyche—not your external circumstances—is the problem.

The pursuit of the truth begins with an unconditional willingness to stick to the seat of the witness and let go of everything that holds you down the moment it hits you. It's invariably more difficult to let go later when you've lost your clarity—when your preoccupation is to rationalize or fix the disturbance.

Key Takeaway: Observe your inner roommate's struggle to be okay and refuse to participate in it.

When you have a thorn in your flesh, you can hide and guard it—create a protective shield over it and restructure your life so nothing touches it—or you can take it out. Inner thorns such as loneliness and low self-esteem give you the same choices. You can find ways to feel less lonely or you can weed out the problem from its roots. Even when you find ways or someone to make you feel less lonely, the fear of being alone always lingers. It affects your behavior such that avoiding loneliness becomes the motive of all your interactions.

Part of freeing yourself from your inner disturbances is recognizing that you—as your consciousness—are separate from your thoughts and emotions. Part of freeing yourself is realizing that nothing you do about your external circumstances will ease your internal disturbances.

From the objective center of the Self, you notice that your negative emotions are merely things you experience. When you sit with your inner disturbances long enough, you become comfortable just watching them, you stop playing with them, and you resist the urge to do something about them.

Once you learn to relax and refuse to participate in your psyche's struggle to feel okay, your inner disturbances defuse by themselves.

Key Takeaway: Stop asking your mind to make everything okay to be okay.

Your mind is attuned to noticing and addressing external problems. Solving one external problem does not settle you because of two reasons: the external problem you solve only masks deeper inner disturbances, and your mind consistently finds another external problem to focus on once the initial problem is resolved.

It's easy to think, for example, that you are lonely because your relationships keep breaking down. You may patch up your relationships and become a better friend, but none of your external efforts may abate your feelings of loneliness. It is more likely that you are lonely because you are trying to get people to like you instead of being interested in and genuinely liking them. As long as you don't stop trying to get people to like you, nothing will make you feel less lonely.

Most people don't know how much they suffer mentally and emotionally because they have acclimated to their suffering. You know you are healthy if you don't have to think about your psyche—about how to be less fearful, less lonely, or less unloved.

You can live through life without your perpetual worries and anxieties when you stop demanding your mind to control people, the things that happen to you, and the insecurities they cause you—because it can't. Observe as it suggests what you have to do to make things better inside and resist the urge to go along with its suggestions. Catch it trying to make things okay and disengage your focus from its thoughts. Don't stop it; just relax, watch, and release. The objective is to become the observer, not the facilitator, of your thoughts.

"The truth is, everything will be okay as soon as you are okay with everything. And that's the only time everything will be okay" (p. 95).

Key Takeaway: Embrace your inner pain to accelerate your spiritual growth.

Any meaningful change is a painful experience. Change is neither new nor meaningful if it does not uproot you from what is familiar and comfortable.

Most of your behaviors, from the clothes you wear to the way you talk, are about avoiding pain—usually the pain of rejection or low self-esteem. Yet anything you do to avoid pain leads you to the pain itself. If you wear certain clothes to avoid the pain of not fitting in, you will feel the pain when someone disparages your outfit. The disparaging comment doesn't cause your pain; it merely stimulates the pain you have been avoiding.

The only way to free yourself from your inner pain is to untether your inner roommate and make peace with your insecurities, jealousy, and other inner disturbances. Don't resist, withdraw or try to protect yourself from the pain; observe the disturbances as changes in your energy flow, relax your heart, and let the blocked energies pass through.

Accept your inner pain, feel it, and observe it as it passes. It's the only way to spiritual freedom.

PART IV:
GOING BEYOND

Key Takeaway: Break the walls that lay a siege on your consciousness to find true freedom.

Your consciousness is hidden by your wall of thoughts and emotions, your self-concept, your beliefs, your past experiences, and your dreams of the future. If something challenges any of these abstracts and you respond defensively, you are not defending yourself; you are defending your walls.

True freedom, or enlightenment, is only found beyond these walls. The only way to get to it is to bring down the walls that lock it in.

Key Takeaway: Disbelieve your mental model to find true spirituality.

True spirituality lies beyond the finite limit of your mental model. It awaits in the infinite freedom that is your consciousness.

To go beyond your restricted self, you have to question and disbelieve your mental model. You have to see your mental model for what it is—a weak façade that you put up to filter reality and give yourself a false sense of control. It's easy to realize the frailty of your mental model, especially when you consider how easily circumstances that defy your expectations shake your self-concept. The weakness of its foundation also becomes obvious when you stop doing the things that make you comfortable—from the way you dress and eat to the way you socialize. When you stop doing the things that keep you in your comfort zone, you are forced to confront the real reason for doing them.

Your mental model is reinforced by your thoughts and behaviors, not by reality, but it influences your reality. The only reason you get angry, anxious, or fearful is because your mental model doesn't accommodate what is happening to you or around you.

You free yourself when you go beyond everything that makes you uncomfortable. It is the fear of the unknown, the discomfort of stepping out, that keeps people in the cage of their mental models.

You can get used to the discomfort of breaking free by stepping toward the edges of your fear, insecurity, or envy a little every day. Little by little, you learn to relax when people or circumstances tug at your insecurities.

Key Takeaway: Let go of your self-concept to find your true, free, and secure self.

Your consciousness chooses what to concentrate on and what to let pass through. When it concentrates on selective thoughts, emotions, or external objects long enough, they become a source of stability in a world of impermanence. As more thoughts, emotions, and objects pile up, they form a structure that you cling to. It is this inner structure that makes up your conceptual self. No matter how elaborate this conceptual self is, it is not you. Your gender, career, dreams, and beliefs make up a conceptual self that only conceals your real Self.

When you center yourself in your consciousness, you let go of your impressions of people, things, and circumstances. Letting go of your self-concept immerses you in the purest form of life. When you let go, you are no longer building mental models to make sense of life. Instead, you are letting the moments pass without trying to control or hold on to their memory, without using them to form impressions. In this clarity, you lose the need to continually defend your remodeled reality and your beliefs. When you go beyond the false part of you, nothing that happens unsettles you.

Your self-concept doesn't defend you; it imprisons you. To let go, remind yourself that you are just the observer of the world and your thoughts. Observe yourself observing your inner disturbances and they will pass.

PART V:
LIVING LIFE

Key Takeaway: Commit to stay open to find and sustain happiness.

Happiness is always within your reach—as long as you don't attach conditions to it. If you commit to being happy regardless of what happens, you are on your way to making an inner breakthrough to complete freedom. And if you can hold on to that commitment when markets crash, when people reject you, or when you suffer catastrophic loss, you can find true spirituality.

Part of being happy is letting go of the part of you that finds reasons to be unhappy. Commit to enjoy life, to learn from and have fun with whatever it throws your way, and to be happy every day.

Everyday happiness comes from a commitment to keep your heart open—to let go of anger, jealousy, envy, and other negative energies the moment they start piling up. Catch yourself closing, observe the negative energies, and remind yourself that your thoughts and emotions are not you. Practicing meditation helps ground you in your consciousness.

Key Takeaway: Nonresistance is the path to inner peace.

Stress, anxiety, and tension are manifestations of a mind that resists the reality of life. When you react to things that have already happened, what you are actually resisting are the mental impressions the experience is leaving on you. In this sense, you are in conflict with yourself, not with the situation. Resistance blocks energy flows and weighs you down. If these energy flows are blocked for too long, they undermine your ability to deal with future events.

When you are present, when all you do is observe and experience life as it unfolds, you experience peace. You can learn to stop resisting and blocking your energy flows by watching your self-concept when it expresses a dislike for something. Will yourself to relax and let the impressions created by a situation pass through before you decide to deal with it.

When acceptance precedes action, you gain the clarity that enables you to deal with the situation, not with the impressions it cues. Acceptance allows you to channel the energy that would have been spent in dealing with fear and desire to dealing with the actual situation.

Key Takeaway: Regularly reflect on death to gain perspective.

Death is a master teacher and the source of human meaning. Contemplating its unpredictability—the fact that it may come to you at any place and time—puts the problems you think you have in perspective. Reflecting on death nudges you to work toward your greatest potential, to surround yourself with love, to think critically about your desires, and to set your priorities right.

Make a habit of considering what you would do with your last week alive. Ask yourself why you would live any other way, considering this week could actually be your last week. You don't have to make any major changes; you just have to find ways to live fully—give up the fear and need for control, be present in every moment, and enjoy small pleasures the way a person with a week to live would.

Reflecting on death is not a call to pursue more experiences; it is a call to find more depth in the experiences you already have.

Key Takeaway: Stick to the middle way to find and sustain clarity.

The Tao, or middle way, is the balance between the extremes of everything—relationships, food, work, action, and inaction. Like a pendulum, nothing in life can remain in the extremes for long. Anything grounded in the center can remain there eternally, and it can do so in peaceful harmony.

The extremes waste your energy—both as you pursue them and as you deal with their consequences. If you commit to eat just enough to stay healthy, you don't have to avoid food or find more of it, and you don't have to struggle with being under- or overweight. When you live at the extremes, you exhaust the energy you would use to move and grow.

Living in the center simplifies and clarifies life. To bring yourself to the center, stop channeling your energy into the extremes. Watch your energy drift to the extreme when something infuriates you or unsettles you in some other way.

As long as you don't follow it there, it will come back to the center.

Key Takeaway: Release your conceptual self to move toward your spiritual being.

When you move toward your consciousness, you move toward the Spirit, toward God. The more you move toward this Self, the more you move away from anger, envy, tension, and other forms of negativity. The negativity may still linger, but as long as all you do is observe it and let it pass, it has no hold on your Self.

When you move away from your psyche and toward the Spirit, the differentiations and judgments you used to make fade away and your heart fills with love, openness, and gratitude.

As you drift further and further from your personal self, you become one with the light of the universe. If you can look at everyone with unconditional love, compassion, and understanding; if you can rise above your thoughts and emotions and see perfection in everything around you, you are looking through the eyes of God.

EDITORIAL REVIEW

In his book *The Untethered Soul: The Journey Beyond Yourself*, Michael A. Singer argues that anyone can transcend his personal self and awaken to the freedom, peace, and joy of true spirituality by realizing that he is not his thoughts, emotions, or beliefs and refusing to participate in his mind's struggle to be okay.

Singer begins by walking the reader through simple thought experiments that illustrate the nature of the true Self—the consciousness or Spirit—as the experiencer and manipulator of thoughts and emotions. He explores the energies that feed emotional states, their sources, and their influence on well-being. Part of his main contention is that people consciously choose to open and close their energy flows by either letting moments pass through them like trees on a highway or clinging onto them. Singer argues that how much people open or close determines how much love, joy, harmony, and gratitude they experience and how much inner disturbance they suffer.

Singer explains that individuals can only find inner peace by letting go of what he calls "disturbed energy patterns"—the fear, anger, envy, and insecurities stored within—and releasing the impressions that situations leave on them the moment they recognize them. He recommends following this release with a commitment to enjoy life and to be unconditionally happy.

Singer adds that true freedom lies beyond the self-concept— beyond what the individual thinks he is, beyond his understanding of the past and his expectations of the future.

It is the individual who releases his self-concept and embraces the ambiguity of a chaotic world—Singer contends—who finds true security and peace.

Singer delivers *The Untethered Soul* in a simple narrative that the lay reader can easily follow. Although some of the ideas—especially about energy flows and inner disturbances—initially appear convoluted, everything ties together into a powerful message in the end.

Since the book is meant to help the reader make a personal exploration of his self, it limits its illustrations to fictitious but assessable examples and selected yogi and biblical texts. Singer does not tie any science to the ideas or practices he proposes, but this should fool no one into thinking this is all spiritual moonshine.

The ideas Singer proposes are closely related to the premises of Acceptance and Commitment Therapy (ACT)—a form of psychotherapy that uses acceptance and mindfulness to increase psychological flexibility. ACT helps patients be present in everyday life, open up to unpleasant circumstances and feelings and, ultimately, get closer to the truth—what *The Untethered Soul* and other spiritual texts call enlightenment. The importance of stepping back from the thinking and feeling self has also been a long-established process in psychotherapy and ancient practices such as yoga.

Unlike ACT—which encourages patients to label and call out negative thoughts and feelings until they dissipate—*The Untethered Soul* is ambiguous on actionable advice. Singer advises readers to "get rid of that part" without following through with a clear "how." His universal solution to inner turmoil seems to be to "simply relax and be aware," and its cousins: "just relax and open," and "relax and release."

Arguably, the reason Singer does not follow through with practical practices for helping the reader go beyond his Self is because that was never his intention. He sets out to make the reader understand why—why the voice inside his head is the source of his suffering, why he needs to defuse his consciousness from his conceptual self, and why everything follows a commitment to be aware. On this intention, Singer delivers in a relatable and mind-provoking way.

ABOUT THE AUTHORS

Michael A. Singer is an American author and founder of the Temple of the Universe—a nonprofit yoga and meditation center. He has authored two other books that focus on the integration of Western and Easter philosophy.

THE END

If you enjoyed this summary, please leave an honest review on Amazon.com...it'd mean a lot to us.

If you haven't already, we encourage you to purchase a copy of the original book.

67269462R00018

Made in the USA
San Bernardino, CA
20 January 2018